Contents

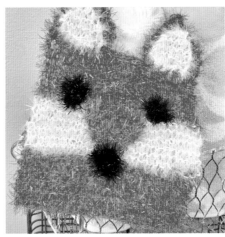

tomato scrubby

Designed by Rebecca J. Venton

Easy

MATERIALS

Yarn 4

RED HEART® Scrubby™, solids 3.5 oz (100 g), 92 yd (85 m), prints 3.0 oz (85 g) 78 yds (71 m) balls
• 1 ball each 905 Cherry A and 620 Lime B

Needles

Susan Bates® Double Pointed Knitting Needles:
5mm [US 8]

Notions

Yarn needle

GAUGE

Gauge is not critical for this project.

FINISHED SIZE

Scrubby measures 6" [15 cm] x 4½" [11.5 cm].

SPECIAL TECHNIQUE

kfb (knit into front and back): Knit next stitch but do not remove from needle, knit into back loop of same stitch and remove from needle.

LEARN BY VIDEO

www.go-crafty.com
kfb (knit into front and back of stitch)

TOMATO

With A, cast on 6 sts.
Row 1: Knit.
Row 2: (Kfb) twice, k2, (kfb) twice – 10 sts.
Row 3: Knit.
Row 4: (Kfb) twice, k6, (kfb) twice – 14 sts.
Row 5: Knit.
Row 6: (Kfb) twice, k10, (kfb) twice – 18 sts.
Row 7: Knit.
Row 8: (Kfb) twice, k14, (kfb) twice – 22 sts.
Row 9: Knit.
Row 10: (Kfb) twice, k18, (kfb) twice – 26 sts.
Rows 11-32: Knit.
Row 33: (K2tog) twice, k18, (k2tog) twice – 22 sts.
Row 34: Knit.
Row 35: (K2tog) twice, k14, (k2tog) twice – 18 sts.
Row 36: Knit.
Row 37: (K2tog) twice, k10, (k2tog) twice – 14 sts.
Row 38: Knit.
Row 39: (K2tog) twice, k6, (k2tog) twice – 10 sts.
Row 40: Knit.
Row 41: (K2tog) twice, k2, (k2tog) twice – 6 sts.
Bind off.

STEM

With B, cast on 8 sts.
[Bind off until 1 st remains on needle, cast on 7 sts] 4 times, bind off all sts, leaving a long tail.

FINISHING

With long tail, fold Stem piece so there are 5 sections and sew together. Sew Stem to top of Tomato. Weave in ends.•

simple knit scrubby

Designed by Laura Bain

Beginner

MATERIALS

Yarn
RED HEART® Scrubby™, solids 3.5 oz (100 g), 92 yd (85 m), prints 3.0 oz (85 g) 78 yds (71 m) balls
• 1 ball 510 Glacier OR 715 Primrose

Needles
Susan Bates® Knitting Needles:
5mm [US 8]

Notions
Yarn needle

GAUGE
Gauge is not critical for this project.

FINISHED SIZE
Washcloth measures approximately 8" [20.5 cm] wide x 7" [18 cm] long

WASHCLOTH
Cast on 30 stitches.
Rows 1-6: Knit.
Row 7: Knit 3, purl 24, knit 3.
Row 8: Knit.
Repeat Rows 7-8 until piece measures 6" [15 cm] from beginning, end with Row 8.
Repeat Rows 1-6.
Bind off.

FINISHING
Weave in ends.•

simple knit dishcloth

Designed by Lorna Miser

Beginner

MATERIALS

Yarn
RED HEART® Scrubby™, solids 3.5 oz (100 g), 92 yd (85 m), prints 3.0 oz (85 g) 78 yds (71 m) balls

- 1 ball 12 Black or 501 Ocean

Needles
Susan Bates® Knitting Needles:
5mm [US 8]

Notions
Yarn needle

GAUGE
16 sts = 4" [10 cm]; 34 rows = 4" [10 cm] in Garter stitch. *CHECK YOUR GAUGE.*
Use any size needles to obtain the gauge.

FINISHED SIZE
7½" [19 cm] square

DISHCLOTH
Cast on 30 sts.
Knit every row until Dishcloth measures 7½» [19 cm] from beginning.
Bind off.

FINISHING
Weave in ends.●

wise owl scrubby

Designed by Michele Wilcox

Easy

MATERIALS

Yarn
RED HEART® Scrubby™, solids 3.5 oz (100 g), 92 yd (85 m), prints 3.0 oz (85 g) 78 yds (71 m) balls
• 1 ball each 905 Cherry A, 010 Coconut B, 561 Grape C, 0241 Duckie D

Needles
Susan Bates® Double Pointed Knitting Needles:
5mm [US 8]

Notions
Yarn needle

GAUGE
Gauge is not critical for this project.

FINISHED SIZE
Scrubby measures 7½" x 7½" (19 x 19 cm)

SPECIAL TECHNIQUE

kfb (knit into front and back): Knit next stitch but do not remove from needle, knit into back loop of same stitch and remove from needle.

LEARN BY VIDEO
www.go-crafty.com
kfb (knit into front and back of stitch)

SCRUBBY

Square
With A, cast on 29 sts.
Row 1: P1, *k3, p1; repeat from * across.
Row 2: K2, *p1, k3, repeat from * to last 3 sts, p1, k2.
Repeat Rows 1 and 2 until piece measures 7½" (19 cm). Bind off loosely.

Eye (make 2)
With B, cast on 6 sts.

Row 1: Kfb in each st—12 sts.
Row 2: Knit.
Row 3: *K1, kfb; repeat from * across—18 sts.
Row 4: Knit.
Row 5: *K2, kfb; repeat from * across—24 sts.
Row 6: Knit.
Row 7: *K3, kfb; repeat from * across—30 sts.
Row 8: Knit.
Row 9: *K4, kfb; repeat from * across—36 sts. Bind off loosely. Shape into a circle and seam across radius. With C, embroider satin st pupils in center. Using photograph as a guide, sew in place.

Beak
With D, cast on 8 sts.
Rows 1 and 2: Knit.
Row 3: K2tog, k4, k2tog—6 sts.
Rows 4 and 5: Knit.
Row 6: K2tog, k2, k2tog—4 sts.
Rows 7 and 8: Knit.
Row 9: [K2tog] twice—2 sts.
Row 10: K2tog—1 st. Bind off, leaving a long tail for sewing. Center beak between eyes and sew in place.

FINISHING
Weave in ends.●

Designed by Nancy Anderson

Easy

MATERIALS

Yarn

RED HEART® Scrubby™, solids 3.5 oz (100 g), 92 yd (85 m), prints 3.0 oz (85 g) 78 yds (71 m) balls
• 1 skein each 905 Cherry A, 10 Coconut B, 12 Black C

Yarn

RED HEART® Super Saver®, solids 7 oz (198 g), 364 yds (333 m); prints, multis and heathers 5 oz (141 g), 236 yds (215 m); flecks 5 oz (141 g), 260 yds (238 m) skeins
• 1 skein 324 Bright Yellow D

Needles
Susan Bates® Knitting Needles: 5 mm [US 8]

Notions
Black sewing thread
Sewing needle
Yarn needle
Yarn Bobbins

GAUGE
18 sts = 4" [10 cm]; 24 rows = 4" [10 cm] in Garter Stitch. *CHECK YOUR GAUGE.* Use any size needle to obtain the gauge.

FINISHED SIZE
Santa Belly Scrubby measures: 7" x 6½" (18 x 16 cm)

PATTERN STITCHES
Garter Stitch
Row 1 (Right Side): K all sts.
Row 2 (Wrong Side): K all sts.
Repeat rows 1-2.

NOTES
Belt is worked separately then attached to surface of fabric with

sewing needle and thread. Belt Buckle is worked in Garter stitch Intarsia, to avoid carrying yarn across back of work, wind 2 bobbins with D. When working in Intarsia and changing colors, remember to twist yarn on Wrong Side to prevent holes in work.

SCRUBBY
With A, cast on 27 sts.
Rows 1-18: Knit.
Rows 19-28: Change to B and Knit.
Rows 29-46: Change to A and Knit.
Next Row: Bind off all stitches.

BELT
With C, cast on 8 stitches
Rows 1-15: Knit.
Rows 16-19: Change to D and knit, carrying C across back of work.
Rows 20-29: Using first bobbin of D, knit 2 stitches, change to C and knit 4 stitches, add second bobbin of D and knit last 2 stitches using D. Repeat for 10 rows.
Rows 30-33: With D from one of the bobbins, knit for 4 rows.
Rows 34-48: With C, knit for 15 rows.
Next Row: Bind off all stitches loosely.

Attaching Belt to Scrubby
With the white stripe running vertically, sew belt securely to Right Side of front mid-section of Scrubby using sewing needle and sewing thread.

FINISHING
Weave in ends.●

scrubby monster mitt

Designed by Laura Bain

Easy

MATERIALS

Yarn (4)
RED HEART® Scrubby™, solids 3.5 oz (100 g), 92 yd (85 m), prints 3.0 oz (85 g) 78 yds (71 m) balls
• 1 ball each 241 Duckie A, 501 Ocean B, 709 Bubblegum C, 10 Coconut D, 12 Black E

Needles
Susan Bates® Circular Knitting Needles: 5.5 mm [US 9] 16" [40 cm]

Notions
Stitch Marker
Yarn needle

GAUGE

18 sts = 4" [10 cm]; 16 rows = 4" [10 cm] in Garter Stitch (knit every row). Gauge is not critical for this pattern. *CHECK YOUR GAUGE.* Use any size needle to obtain the gauge.

FINISHED SIZE

Mitt measures: 9" [23 cm] long x 4" [10 cm] wide.

SPECIAL ABBREVIATIONS

kfb (knit into front and back): Knit next stitch but do not remove from needle, knit into back loop of same stitch and remove from needle.

k2tog Knit 2 stitches together (decrease)..

LEARN BY VIDEO
www.go-crafty.com
kfb (knit into front and back of stitch)
k2tog (knit 2 stitches together)

MONSTER MITT

With A, cast on 48 sts. Join, being careful not to twist stitches and place stitch marker to mark beginning of round.
Round 1: *K2, P2*, repeat from * to * to end of round.
Next Rounds: Repeat Round 1 until piece measures 2" [5 cm] from cast on edge.
Next Rounds: Knit every round for 1" [2.5 cm], cut yarn.
Next Rounds: Change to B, knit every round until pieces measures 6" [15 cm] from cast on edge, cut yarn.
Next Rounds: Change to C, knit every round until piece measures 9" [23 cm] from cast on edge.
Next Round: Bind off all stitches loosely.

EYE

With E, cast on 8 stitches.
Row 1: KFB in each stitch — 16 sts.
Row 2: KFB, *K1, KFB*, ending with K1 — 24 sts, cut yarn.
Row 3: Change to D. KFB, *K2, KFB*, ending with K2 — 32 sts.
Row 4: Bind off all stitches loosely.
With Yarn Needle, join ends together and sew Eye into a circle, set aside.

MOUTH

With E, cast on 12 stitches.
Row 1: Knit.
Row 2: Bind off all stitches loosely.
Using D, pick up and knit 4 stitches on each side of mouth.
Row 1: Knit 4 stitches.
Row 2: K2tog, knit — 3 sts.
Row 3: K2tog, knit — 2 sts.
Row 4: K2tog — 1 st.
Cut yarn and thread through remaining stitch and tie off.

FINISHING

Using Yarn Needle, Sew top seam together and weave in all tails and loose ends.

Eye
With Yarn Needle, sew "Eye" to top/center of mitt. Center the "Eye" over B and C in the middle of the mitt. Use photo as a guide for placement.

Mouth
With Yarn Needle, sew "Mouth" to middle of mitt over B. Center "Mouth" under the "Eye", about 1½" [3.8 cm] apart. Use photo as a guide for placement.•

striped knit scrubby dishcloth

Designed by Bobbi Anderson

Easy

MATERIALS

Yarn

RED HEART® Scrubby™, solids 3.5 oz (100 g), 92 yd (85 m), prints 3.0 oz (85 g) 78 yds (71 m) balls
• 1 ball each: 620 Lime A, 940 Capri B

Needles
Susan Bates® Knitting Needles:
5mm [US 8]

Notions
Yarn needle

GAUGE

14.5 sts = 4" [10 cm]; 27.5 rows = 4" [10 cm] in Striped sequence.
Exact gauge is not crucial for this project.

FINISHED SIZE

Dishcloth measures 7" [18 cm] wide x 7" [18 cm] long

NOTE
When changing yarn, do not cut; carry yarn not used loosely up the side of your work.

DISHCLOTH
With A, loosely cast on 26 stitches.
Work in the following color and stitch sequence:
*Rows 1-6: Starting with a Right Side row, using A, work 6 rows in Garter St.
Rows 7-12: Change to B and work 6 rows in Stockinette St.
Repeat from * 3 more times (Dishcloth will measure 7" [18 cm]).
With B, loosely bind off all sts.

FINISHING
Weave in all ends.•

striped sparkle scrubby

Designed by Nancy Anderson

Easy

MATERIALS

Yarn
RED HEART® Scrubby Sparkle™, solids 3 oz (85g), 174 yd (159m) balls
• 1 ball each 8830 Blueberry A, and 8506 Icepop B.

Needles
Susan Bates® Knitting Needles:
5mm [US 8]

Notions
Yarn needle

GAUGE
18 sts = 4" [10 cm]; 27 rows = 4" [10 cm] in Garter stitch (knit every row). *CHECK YOUR GAUGE.* Use any size needles to obtain the gauge given.

FINISHED SIZE
Scrubby measures about 6" x 6" [15 x 15 cm].

NOTES
1 These super simple scrubby dish cloths are worked in Garter stitch (knit every row), changing color every two rows to form stripes.
2 When changing color, do not cut old yarn color until instructed. Carry color not in use loosely up side of piece until next needed.

DISHCLOTH 1
With A, cast on 27 sts.
Row 1: With A, knit.
Join B.
Drop, but do not cut A. Carry color not in use loosely up side of piece.
Rows 2 and 3: With B, knit.
Drop, but do not cut B.

Rows 4 and 5: With A, knit.
Rows 6–37: Repeat Rows 2–5 eight more times. Notes: The last row you work will be a 2nd row worked with A. You will have a total of nineteen stripes from beginning: ten A-colored stripes and nine B-colored stripes.
Drop, but do not cut A.
Rows 38 and 39: With B, knit.
Cut B, leaving a tail to weave in later.
Row 40: With A, knit.
With A, bind off loosely.

DISHCLOTH 2
Make same as Dish Cloth I, reversing the yarn colors.

FINISHING
Weave in ends.•

candy corn scrubby

Designed by Michele Wilcox

Easy

MATERIALS

Yarn (4)
RED HEART® Scrubby Sparkle™, solids 3
oz (85g), 78 yd (71m) balls
• 1 ball each 8001 Marshmallow A, 8260
Orange B, 8215 Lemon C

Needles
Susan Bates® Knitting Needles:
4 mm [US 6]

Notions
Yarn Needle

GAUGE

18 sts = 4" [10 cm]; 24 rows = 4" [10 cm]
in Garter Stitch (knit every row). Gauge is
not critical for this pattern.
CHECK YOUR GAUGE. Use any size
needle to obtain the gauge.

FINISHED SIZE

Candy Corn Scrubby measures: 7"x 7¼"
[18 x 18 cm]

SPECIAL TECHNIQUE

M1 Make 1 (Increase): Lift strand between needles to left-hand
needle and knit strand through the back loop, twisting it to
prevent a hole.

LEARN BY VIDEO
www.go-crafty.com
M1L (Make 1 Left)

SCRUBBY

With A, cast on 7 sts.
Row 1: Knit.

Row 2: K1, M1, knit across row to last stitch, M1, K1—9 sts.
Rows 3-16: Repeat Rows 1-2. At end of Row 16, cut yarn
leaving a 3" [8 cm] tail—23 sts.
Row 17: Change to B and knit.
Row 18: Repeat Row 2—25 sts.
Rows 19-36: Repeat Rows 1-2. At end of
Row 36, cut yarn cut yarn leaving a 3" [8 cm]
tail —43 sts.
Rows 37-55: Change to C and knit every Row.
Row 56: Bind off all stitches loosely

FINISHING

Using yarn needle, weave in all tails and loose ends.•

wrap it up gift scrubby

Designed by Rebecca J. Venton

Easy

MATERIALS

Yarn
RED HEART® Scrubby Sparkle™, solids 3 oz (85g), 174 yd (159m) balls
• 1 ball each 8690 Avocado A and 8929 Strawberry B

Needles
Susan Bates® Knitting Needles:
5mm [US 8]

Notions
Yarn needle

GAUGE

Gauge is not critical for this project.

FINISHED SIZE

Scrubby measures 6" x 6" (15 x 15 cm).

GIFT BOX

With A, cast on 27 sts.
Knit every row until piece measures 6" (15 cm).
Bind off all sts.

RIBBONS (make 2)

With B, cast on 27 sts, and knit 3 rows.
Bind off all sts.

BOW TIE

With B, cast on 45 sts, and knit 3 rows.
Bind off all sts.

FINISHING

With A, sew Ribbons to Gift Box, centering one ribbon vertically and the other horizontally across box. Tie Bow Tie piece into a bow, and sew to center of Gift Box with B.
Weave in all loose ends.•

fish-time scrubbing mitt

Designed by Lorna Miser

Intermediate

MATERIALS

Yarn

RED HEART® Scrubby™, solids 3.5 oz (100 g), 92 yd (85 m), prints 3.0 oz (85 g) 78 yds (71 m) balls
• 1 ball each 905 Cherry A and 709 Bubblegum

Needles
Susan Bates® Double Pointed Knitting 5mm [US 8]

Notions
Stitch markers
Yarn needle

GAUGE

16 sts = 4" [10 cm]; 34 rows = 4" [10 cm] in Garter stitch. *CHECK YOUR GAUGE.*
Use any size needles to obtain the gauge.

FINISHED SIZE

7½" [19 cm] circumference

NOTES

Carry colors not in use loosely along wrong side of work, twisting colors every other row to prevent long floats.

DISHCLOTH

With A, cast on 60 sts. Join to work in the round, taking care not to twist sts. Place marker for beginning of round.
[Knit 1 round. Purl 1 round] for Garter st until piece measures 1½" [4 cm] from beginning. Do not cut yarn.
Next Round: Join B, [k2tog] around – 30 sts.
Work 9 more rounds in Garter stitch, carrying A along inside and twisting every other round.
Change to A and work 10 rounds in Garter st, carrying B along inside.
Change to B and work 10 rounds in Garter st, carrying A along inside.
Change to A and work 10 rounds in Garter st, carrying B along inside. Cut A.

SHAPE TIP

Decrease Round: With B, [k1, k2tog] around—20 sts. Work in Garter st for 5 rounds.

Decrease Round: [K2tog] around—10 sts.
Work in Garter st for 3 rounds. Cut yarn leaving a long tail.
Thread tail through all remaining sts twice. Pull to gather and knot end securely.

FINISHING
Weave in ends.●

corner-to-corner dishcloth

Designed by Bobbi Anderson

Easy

MATERIALS

Yarn (4)
RED HEART® Scrubby™, solids 3.5 oz (100 g), 92 yd (85 m), prints 3.0 oz (85 g) 78 yds (71 m) balls
• 1 ball: 980 Tropical

Needles
Susan Bates® Knitting Needles: 5mm [US 8]

Notions
Yarn needle

GAUGE
14.5 sts = 4" [10 cm]; 30 rows = 4" [10 cm] in Garter st.
Exact gauge is not crucial for this project.

FINISHED SIZE
Dishcloth measures 7" [18 cm] wide x 7" [18 cm] long

SPECIAL TECHNIQUES
kfb (knit front and back): Knit into the front of next stitch and leave on left needle; knit into the back of same stitch and drop both stitches from left needle - increase made.
SKP (slip, knit, pass over): Slip next stitch knitwise to right needle; knit stitch on left needle; pass slipped stitch over knit stitch and off right needle - decrease made.

LEARN BY VIDEO|
www.go-crafty.com
kfb (knit into front and back of stitch)
SKP (slip 1, knit 1, pass slip stitch over)

DISHCLOTH
Cast on 2 sts.
Row 1: Kfb, knit 1 – 3 sts.
Row 2: Knit 1, kfb, knit 1 – 4 sts.
Increase Row: Knit 1, kfb, knit to end of row – 5 sts.
Repeat Increase Row until there are 37 sts on needle.
Decrease Row: Knit 1, skp, knit to end of row – 36 sts.
Repeat Decrease Row until there are 2 sts on needle.
Final Row: Skp.
Fasten off last st.

FINISHING
Weave in all ends.•

garter stitch round scrubby

Designed by Rebecca J. Venton

Easy

MATERIALS

Yarn
RED HEART® Scrubby Cotton®, solids 3.5 oz (100 g) 145 yd (133 m), prints 3 oz (85 g) 128 yd (117 m) balls
• 1 ball 7933 Paradise Print

Needles
Susan Bates® Knitting Needles: 5mm [US 8]

Notions
Yarn needle

GAUGE
17 sts = 4" [10 cm]; 21 rows = 4" [10 cm] in Garter Stitch (knit every row). Gauge is not critical for this pattern.
CHECK YOUR GAUGE. Use any size needle to obtain the gauge.

FINISHED SIZE
Scrubby measures: 6" x 6" [15 x 15 cm] in diameter.

PATTERN STITCH
Garter Stitch
Row 1 (Right Side): K all sts.
Row 2 (Wrong Side): K all sts.
Repeat rows 1-2.

SCRUBBY
Cast on 9 sts. This is the foundation row.
Row 1: K3 sts; turn.
Row 2: K3 sts; turn.
Row 3: K6 sts; turn.
Row 4: K6 sts; turn.
Row 5: K9 sts; turn.
Row 6: K9 sts; turn.
Repeat Rows 1-6, 23 more times.
Next Row: Bind off all stitches, leaving a 12" [30 cm] long tail.

FINISHING
Thread tail through Yarn Needle. Use a running stitch along center edge of work, pull tightly, then sew cast on edge to bound off edge. Draw yarn through remaining st twice; fasten securely. Weave in all ends.•

lucky lady bug scrubby

Designed by Rebecca J. Venton

Easy

MATERIALS

Yarn 4

RED HEART® Scrubby™, solids 3.5 oz (100 g), 92 yd (85 m), prints 3.0 oz (85 g) 78 yds (71 m) balls
• 1 ball each 905 Cherry A and 12 Black B

Needles
Susan Bates® Knitting Needles:
5mm [US 8]

Notions
Stitch markers
Yarn needle

GAUGE
Gauge is not critical for this project.

FINISHED SIZE
Scrubby measures 6" [15 cm] wide x 7" [18 cm] long.

SPECIAL TECHNIQUE
kfb (knit into front and back): Knit next stitch but do not remove from needle, knit into back loop of same stitch and remove from needle.

LEARN BY VIDEO
www.go-crafty.com
kfb (knit into front and back of stitch).

BODY
With A, cast on 3 sts.
Row 1: Kfb in each st – 6 sts.
Row 2: Knit.
Row 3: Kfb in each st – 12 sts.
Row 4: Knit.
Row 5: [Kfb, k1] 6 times – 18 sts.
Row 6: K1, [place marker, k2] 8 times, place marker, k1.
Row 7: [Knit to 1 st before marker, kfb, slip marker] 8 times, knit to end – 26 sts.
Row 8: Knit.
Repeat Rows 7-8 until piece measures 3" [7.5 cm] from beginning. Bind off, leaving a long tail for sewing.

DOTS (make 6)
With B, cast on 3 sts.
Row 1: Kfb, k1, kfb – 5 sts.
Row 2: Knit.
Row 3: K2tog, k1, k2tog – 3 sts.
Bind off, leaving long tail.

HEAD
With B, cast on 8 sts.
Rows 1-3: Knit.
Row 4: K2tog, k4, k2tog – 6 sts.
Row 5: Knit.
Row 6: K2tog, k2, k2tog – 4 sts.
Row 7: [K2tog] twice – 2 sts.
Bind off, leaving long tail.

ANTENNA
With B, cast on 6 sts.
Bind off, leaving long tail.

FINISHING
Using long tails and following photo, sew side edges of Body together to make a circle.
Using 2 strands of B, backstitch down center of Body.
Sew Dots to Body. Sew Head to Body. Sew center of Antennae to top of Head.
Weave in ends.•

clean in stripes dishcloth

Designed by Michele Wilcox

Easy

MATERIALS

Yarn 【4】
RED HEART® Scrubby™, solids 3.5 oz (100 g), 92 yd (85 m), prints 3.0 oz (85 g) 78 yds (71 m) balls
• 1 ball each of 709 Bubblegum A and 241 Duckie B

Needles
Susan Bates® Knitting Needles: 5mm [US 8]

Notions
Yarn needle

GAUGE

15 sts = 4" (10 cm); 25 rows = 4" (10 cm) in Garter st (knit every row) *CHECK YOUR GAUGE*. Use any size needles to obtain the gauge.

FINISHED SIZE

Cloth measures 7" x 7" (18 x 18 cm) square.

NOTES

Color is changed to form stripes. Carry color not in use carefully up side of piece.

TREE

With A, cast on 26 sts.
Work in Garter st (knit every row), changing color as in the following sequence: [Work 4 rows with A, 2 rows with B, 2 rows with A, 2 rows with B] 4 times, then work 4 rows with A.
Bind off loosely.

FINISHING

Weave in ends.•

colorblock knit dishcloth

Designed by Bobbi Anderson

Easy

MATERIALS

Yarn
RED HEART® Scrubby Cotton®, solids 3.5 oz (100 g) 145 yd (133 m), prints 3 oz (85 g) 128 yd (117 m) balls
• 1 ball each: 7586 Jade A, 7939 Tranquil Print B

Needles
Susan Bates® Knitting Needles: 5mm [US 8]

Notions
Yarn needle

GAUGE
14.5 sts = 4" [10 cm]; 27.5 rows = 4" [10 cm] in Stockinette st.
Exact gauge is not crucial for this project.

FINISHED SIZE
Dishcloth measures 7" [18 cm] wide x 7" [18 cm] long

NOTES
1 Divide A into 2 equal balls.
2 When changing yarn within rows, twist the two colors together on Wrong Side to avoid 'holes'.

DISHCLOTH
With first ball of A, loosely cast on 26 stitches.
Knit 7 rows.

INTARSIA SECTION
Note: Join B in next row.
Row 1 (Right Side): With A, knit 6; with B, knit 14; with second ball of A, knit 6.

Row 2 (Wrong Side): With A, knit 6; with B, p14; with A, knit 6.
Repeat Rows 1 & 2 until piece measures 6" [15 cm], ending with a Wrong Side row.
Next Row: With A, knit across all stitches, dropping B and the second ball of A.
Knit 5 rows.
Loosely bind off all sts.

FINISHING
Weave in all ends.•

christmas tree scrubby

Designed by Michele Wilcox

MATERIALS

Yarn
RED HEART® Scrubby™, solids 3.5 oz (100 g), 92 yd (85 m), prints 3.0 oz (85 g) 78 yds (71 m) balls
• 1 ball each 620 Lime A, and 905 Cherry B

Needles
Susan Bates® Knitting Needles:
4mm [US 6]

Susan Bates® Crochet Hook:
6mm [US J-10] (for garland, optional)

Notions
Yarn needle

GAUGE
Gauge is not critical for this project.

FINISHED SIZE
Scrubby measures about 8" [20.5 cm] wide at widest and 9½" [24 cm] long, not including hanging loop.

SPECIAL TECHNIQUE
surface slip st: Hold yarn on back side of piece, insert hook from front to back through fabric and draw up a loop (1 loop on hook), *a short distance from previous insertion point, insert hook from front to back and draw loop through fabric and through loop on hook; repeat from * as desired.

LEARN BY VIDEO
www.go-crafty.com
sl st (slip stitch)

NOTES
1 Tree is worked from the lower edge upwards.
2 Optional garland is worked onto finished tree, using crochet hook and surface slip stitch.

TREE STAND
With B, cast on 16 sts.
Work in Garter stitch (knit every row) until piece measures about 2" [5 cm] from beginning.
Leave stitches on left needle and cut B, leaving a tail about 4" [10 cm] long to weave in later.

TREE
Attach A to first st on left needle.
Row 1: Cast on 10 sts to the left needle, knit across the 10 new sts, knit across the 16 stand sts—26 sts.
Row 2: Cast on 10 sts to the left needle, knit across the 10 new sts, knit across the remaining 26 sts—36 sts.
Rows 3–5: Work in Garter stitch for 3 rows.
Row 6 (decrease row): K2tog, knit to last 2 sts, k2tog—34 sts.
Rows 7–10: Repeat Rows 3–6 once—32 sts.
Rows 11–15: Work in Garter stitch for 5 rows.
Row 16: Repeat Row 6—30 sts.
Rows 17–22: Repeat Rows 11–16—28 sts.
Rows 23–25: Work in Garter stitch for 3 rows.
Row 26: Repeat Row 6—26 sts.
Rows 27–42: Repeat Rows 23–26 four times—18 sts.
Row 43: Knit.
Row 44: Repeat Row 6—16 sts.
Rows 45–50: repeat Rows 43 and 44 three times—10 sts.
Row 51: [K2tog] 5 times—5 sts.
Row 52: K2tog, k1, k2tog—3 sts.
Row 53: K3tog—1 st.
Do not fasten off.

HANGING LOOP
Row 1: Cast on 15 sts for hanging loop, knit the 15 new sts, knit the last st—16 sts.
Bind off, leaving a long tail for sewing.
Sew end of hanging loop to top of tree.

GARLAND (OPTIONAL)
With crochet hook, join B to side of tree near tip. Referring to photograph for placement, work surface slip st zigzag lines back and forth across tree. Keep stitches slightly loose so they stay on the surface.

FINISHING
Weave in ends. ●

zigzag stripes knit dishcloth

Designed by Bobbi Anderson

Easy

MATERIALS

Yarn
RED HEART® Scrubby™, solids 3.5 oz (100 g), 92 yd (85 m), prints 3.0 oz (85 g) 78 yds (71 m) balls
• 1 ball each: 510 Glacier A, 650 Green Tea B, 715 Primrose C

Needles
Susan Bates® Double Pointed Knitting Needles:
5mm [US 8]

Notions
Yarn needle

GAUGE

17 sts = 4" [10 cm]; 20.5 rows = 4" [10 cm] in ZigZag pattern.
Exact gauge is not crucial for this project.

FINISHED SIZE

Dishcloth measures 7" [18 cm] wide x 7" [18 cm] long.

LEARN BY VIDEO

www.go-crafty.com
kfb (knit into front and back of stitch)
skp (slip 1, knit 1, pass slip stitch over)
k2tog (knit 2 stitches together)

NOTE

When changing yarn, do not cut; carry yarn not used, loosely along the side of your work.

SPECIAL TECHNIQUES

kfb (knit into front and back): Knit next stitch but do not remove from needle, knit into back loop of same stitch and remove from needle.

skp (slip, knit, pass over): Slip next stitch knitwise to right needle; knit stitch on left needle; pass slipped stitch over knit stitch and off right needle - left slanting decrease made.

k2tog: Knit 2 stitches together (decrease).

DISHCLOTH

With A, loosely cast on 30 stitches.
Knit 1 Wrong Side row.
Row 1 (Right Side): Knit 1, kfb, knit 4, skp, k2tog, knit 4, [kfb] twice, knit 4, skp, k2tog, knit 4, kfb, knit 1.
Row 2 (Wrong Side): Purl.
Rows 3-6: Repeat Rows 1-2, twice.
Rows 7-12: Change to B and repeat Rows 1-6.
Rows 13-18: Change to C and repeat Rows 1-6.
Repeat Rows 1-18, once.
Loosely bind off all sts.

FINISHING

Weave in all ends.•

loving heart scrubby

Designed by Peggy Greigg

Easy

MATERIALS

Yarn 🔢
RED HEART® Scrubby Cotton®, solids 3.5 oz (100 g) 145 yd (133 m), prints 3 oz (85 g) 128 yd (117 m) balls
• 1 ball 7775 Tulip Pink

Needles
Susan Bates® Knitting Needles:
5mm [US 8]

Notions
Yarn needle

GAUGE
Gauge is not critical for this project.

FINISHED SIZE
Heart Scrubby measures 6" x 6" (15 x 15 cm)

SPECIAL TECHNIQUE
kfb (knit into front and back): Knit next stitch but do not remove from needle, knit into back loop of same stitch and remove from needle.

LEARN BY VIDEO
www.go-crafty.com
kfb (knit into front and back of stitch)

HEART SCRUBBY
Cast on 3 sts.
Knit 1 row.
Row 1: Kfb, knit to end of row – 4 sts.
Repeat Row 1 for 19 more times – 23 sts on last row worked.
Knit every row until piece measures 4½" [11.5 cm] from cast on edge.
Wind a second ball of yarn from original ball.

Make Split for Top of Heart
Row 1: K11, join second ball of yarn and k2tog, k10 – 11 sts each side.
Row 2: Working both sides at same time with separate balls of yarn, k11 for first side; k11 for second side – 11 sts each side.
Row 3: K2tog, k7, k2tog for first side; k2tog, k7, k2tog for second side – 9 sts each side.
Row 4: Knit each side.
Row 5: K2tog, k5, k2tog for first side; k2tog, k5, k2tog for second side – 7 sts each side.
Bind off all stitches each side. Cut yarn.

FINISHING
With yarn needle, weave in ends.•

froggy scrubby

Designed by Michele Wilcox

Easy

MATERIALS

Yarn 4
RED HEART® Scrubby™, solids 3.5 oz (100 g), 92 yd (85 m), prints 3.0 oz (85 g) 78 yds (71 m) balls
• 1 ball of 620 Lime A, 709 Bubblegum B, and 10 Coconut C

Needles
Susan Bates® Knitting Needles:
3.75mm [US 5]

Notions
Small amount of black yarn
Yarn needle

GAUGE
Gauge is not critical for this project.

FINISHED SIZE
Scrubby measures 6½" [16.5 cm] x 6½" [16.5 cm].

SPECIAL TECHNIQUE
kfb (Knit into front and back): Knit next stitch but do not remove from needle, knit into back loop of same stitch and remove from needle.

LEARN BY VIDEO
www.go-crafty.com
kfb (knit into front and back of stitch)

FROGGY FACE
With A, cast on 35 sts.
Row 1: [K2, p2] to last 3 sts, k2, p1.
Repeat Row 1 until piece measures 6½" [16.5 cm] from beginning. Bind off in pattern.

EYE (MAKE 2)
With C, cast on 6 sts.
Row 1: Kfb in each st across – 12 sts.
Row 2: Knit.
Row 3: [K1, kfb] across – 18 sts.
Row 4: Change to A, knit.
Row 5: [K2, kfb] across – 24 sts.
Bind off.
Sew side edges closed to make a circle.

HANGER
With A, cast on 16 sts.
Bind off.
Fold in half, lining up ends. Sew ends in center of top of Face.

TONGUE
With B, cast on 3 sts.
Rows 1-3: Knit.
Row 4: K3tog.
Fasten off, leaving long end.

FINISHING
With Black, embroider pupil in each Eye in satin stitch.
Sew Eye on either side of Face.
Using Black, embroider mouth in straight stitch.
Sew Tongue in corner of mouth.
Weave in ends.•

mitered stripes washcloth

Designed by Jodi Lewanda

Easy

MATERIALS

Yarn
RED HEART® Scrubby Cotton®, solids 3.5 oz (100 g) 145 yd (133 m), prints 3 oz (85 g) 121 yd (110 m) balls
• 4mm [US 6]

Needles
Susan Bates® Knitting Needles:
5 mm [US 8]

Notions
Stitch marker
Yarn needle

GAUGE
Gauge is not critical for this project.

FINISHED SIZE
Scrubby measures 6" [15 cm] wide x 6" [15 cm] long

SPECIAL TECHNIQUE
ssk (1 st decrease): Slip next two stitches knitwise to right needle, insert point of left needle through front of sts, knit these sts together through back loop.

LEARN BY VIDEO
www.go-crafty.com
ssk (slip, slip, knit)

WASHCLOTH
With A, cast on 48 sts.
Row 1 (WS): K24, place marker, knit to end.Z
Row 2: Knit to 2 sts before marker, ssk, slip marker, k2tog, knit to end – 46 sts.
Row 3: Knit.
Row 4: Repeat Row 2 – 44 sts.
Row 5: Knit.
Row 6-11: Change to B and repeat Row 4-5 for 3 times – 38 sts on last row worked.

Rows 12-17: Change to C and repeat Rows 4-5 for 3 times – 32 sts on last row worked.
Rows 18-23: Change to A and repeat Rows 4-5 for 3 times – 26 sts on last row worked.
Rows 24-29: Change to B and repeat Row 4-5 for 3 times – 20 sts on last row worked.
Rows 30-35: Change to C and repeat Rows 4-5 for 3 times – 14 sts on last row worked.
Rows 36-41: Change to A and repeat Rows 4-5 for 3 times – 8 sts on last row worked.
Rows 42-45: Change to B and repeat Row 4-5 for 2 times – 4 sts on last row worked.
Row 46: Ssk, slip marker, k2tog – 2 sts.
Row 47: K2tog.
Fasten off last st.

FINISHING
Weave in ends.•

knit back scrubber

Designed by Michele Wilcox

Easy

MATERIALS

Yarn
RED HEART® Scrubby™, solids 3.5 oz (100 g), 92 yd (85 m), prints 3.0 oz (85 g) 78 yds (71 m) balls
• 1 ball 715 Primrose

Needles
Susan Bates® Knitting Needles:
4.5mm [US 7]

Notions
Yarn needle

GAUGE

16 sts = 4" [10 cm]; 21 rows = 4" [10 cm] in Stockinette Stitch. *CHECK YOUR GAUGE.* Use any size needle to obtain the gauge.

FINISHED SIZE

Back Scrubber measures: 4¾ " width x 22 " length [12 cm x 56 cm]

SPECIAL TECHNIQUES

k2tog: Knit 2 sts together (decrease).
M1: Make 1 stitch (increase).

LEARN BY VIDEO
www.go-crafty.com
k2teg (knit 2 stitches together)
M1L (make 1 left)

PATTERN STITCHES

Seed Stitch
Row 1 (Right Side): *K1, p1; repeat from * to end of row.
Row 2 (Wrong Side): Knit the purl sts, purl the knit stitches.
Repeat Rows 1-2 for Seed Stitch.

Stockinette Stitch
Row 1 (Right Side): Knit all stitches.
Row 2 (Wrong Side): Purl all stitches.
Repeat Rows 1-2 for Stockinette Stitch.

BACK SCRUBBER

Cast on 18 sts.
Row 1 (Right Side): *K2, p2; repeat from * to last 2 sts, k2.
Row 2 (Wrong Side): *P2, k2; repeat from * to last 2 sts, p2.
Next Rows: Repeat Rows1-2 until piece measures 2" [5 cm] from cast-on edge.
Next Row (Right Side): K9, m1, k9—19 sts.
Next Row: Work in Seed St across row, ending K1.
Next Rows: Continue working in Seed Stitch until piece measures 20" [51 cm] from cast on edge.
Next Row: K9, k2tog, k8—18 sts.
Next Rows: Repeat Rows 1-2 until piece measures 22" [56 cm] from cast on edge. Bind off all sts in ribbing.
Next Row: Fold cast-on edge over to meet the end of the 2" [5 cm] K2, P2 ribbing, this creates a "casing" to insert handles through. With yarn and yarn needle, sew cast-on edge to last row of ribbing leaving ends open for inserting handles. Repeat on other end of Scrubber.

HANDLE (Make 2)

Cast on 40 sts.
Row 1 (Right Side): K across row.
Row 2 (Wrong Side): P across row and at same time bind off all sts loosely.

FINISHING

Using a crochet hook, pull handle through casing on end of scrubber. With yarn needle, sew two ends of handle together securely. Repeat on other end of scrubber. Weave in ends.•

coffee mug scrubby

Designed by Nancy Anderson

Easy

MATERIALS

Yarn

RED HEART® Scrubby Sparkle™, solids 3 oz (85g), 78 yd (71m) balls
• 1 ball each 8506 Icepop A, 8001 Marshmallow B and 8690 Avocado C

Needles
Susan Bates® Knitting Needles: 5mm [US 8]

Notions
Yarn needle

GAUGE

Gauge is not critical for this project.

FINISHED SIZE

Scrubby measures 5" [12.5 cm] x 6" [15 cm], excluding handle.

NOTES

Inner Mug section is worked in intarsia. Use separate ball of yarn for each large block of color. Pick up new yarn from under old to twist yarns and prevent holes. Carry colors not in use loosely along wrong side of work.

SPECIAL TECHNIQUES

kfb (knit into front and back): Knit 1 front and back (increase) Knit next st, then knit it through back loop.
ssk: (1 st decrease) Slip next two stitches knitwise to right needle, insert point of left needle through front of sts, knit these sts together through back loop.

LEARN BY VIDEO

www.go-crafty.com
kfb (knit into front and back of stitch)
ssk (slip, slip, knit)

MUG

With A, cast on 20 sts.
Row 1: K2, kfb, k14, kfb, k2—22 sts.
Row 2: K2, kfb, k16, kfb, k2—24 sts.
Row 3: K2, kfb, k18, kfb, k2—26 sts.
Row 4: K2, kfb, k20, kfb, k2—28 sts.
Rows 5-8: Knit. Cut A.
Rows 9-12: Change to B and knit 4 rows. Cut B.
Rows 13-20: Change to A and knit 8 rows. Cut A.
Rows 21-24: Change to B and knit 4 rows. Cut B.
Rows 25-31: Change to A and knit 7 rows. Cut A.
Row 32: K4 with A, change to C and k20, change to A and k4.
Row 33: K3 with A, k22 with C, k3 with A.
Row 34: With A, ssk, k1, k22 with C, with A, k1, k2tog—26 sts.
Row 35: With A, ssk, k22 with C, with A, k2tog – 24 sts.
Row 36: K1 with A, with C, ssk, k18, k2tog, k1 with A—22 sts.
Row 37: K1 with A, with C, ssk, k16, k2tog, k1 with A—20 sts. Cut C.
Row 38: Working with A across all sts, ssk, k16, k2tog—18 sts.
Bind off, working ssk over first 2 sts and k2tog over last 2 sts.

HANDLE

With A, cast on 21 sts.
Rows 1-2: Knit.
Bind off tightly to curve long edge.

FINISHING

Using bind-off edge for curved inner edge, sew short edges of Handle to one side of Mug, about 1½" [4 cm] from top and bottom edges of Mug. Weave in ends.•

spooky stripes scrubby

Designed by Michele Wilcox

Easy

MATERIALS

Yarn (4)
RED HEART® Scrubby™, solids 3.5 oz (100 g), 92 yd (85 m), prints 3.0 oz (85 g) 78 yds (71 m) balls
• 1 skein each 12 Black A, 620 Lime B, 561 Grape C

Needles
Susan Bates® Knitting Needles:
4.5 mm [US 7]

Notions
Yarn needle

GAUGE

17 sts = 4" [10 cm]; 22 rows = 4" [10 cm] in Chevron Stitch Pattern. Gauge is not critical for this pattern. CHECK YOUR GAUGE. Use any size needle to obtain the gauge.

FINISHED SIZE

7½" x 7½" [19 cm x 19 cm]

SPECIAL STITCHES

k3tog: Knit 3 stitches together.
yo: Yarn over needle.

LEARN BY VIDEO

www.go-crafty.com
k3tog (knit 3 stitches together)
yo (yarn over)

PATTERN STITCH

Chevron Stitch Pattern
Row 1: K2, *YO, K5, K3tog, K5, YO, K1, repeat from * to last st, K1.
Row 2: K1, P to last st, K1.
Row 3: Knit.
Row 4: Knit.
Repeat Rows 1-4 for Chevron Stitch Pattern.

SCRUBBY

With A, cast on 31 sts.
Rows 1-4: Work Rows 1-4 of Chevron Stitch Pattern, cut yarn leaving a 3" [8 cm] tail.
Rows 5-8: Change to B and work Rows 1-4 of Chevron Stitch Pattern, cut yarn leaving a 3" [8 cm] tail.
Rows 9-12: Change to C and work Rows 1-4 of Chevron Stitch Pattern, cut yarn leaving a 3" [8 cm] tail.
Rows 13-16: Change to B and work Rows 1-4 of Chevron Stitch Pattern, cut yarn leaving a 3" [8 cm] tail.
Rows 17-20: Change to A and work Rows 1-4 of Chevron Stitch Pattern, cut yarn leaving a 3" [8 cm] tail.
Repeat Rows 5-20, 2 times more.
Next Row: Bind off all stitches loosely.

FINISHING

Using Yarn Needle, weave in all tails and loose ends.•

Designed by Louise Greer

Easy

MATERIALS

Yarn ④
RED HEART® Scrubby Sparkle™, solids 3 oz (85g), 78 yd (71m) balls
• 1 ball each 8001 Marshmallow A and 8929 Strawberry B

Needles
Susan Bates® Knitting Needles:
5mm [US 8]

Notions
Yarn Needle

GAUGE
Gauge is not critical for this project.

FINISHED SIZE
Mitt measures 4¾" [12 cm] wide by 8" [20.5 cm] long.

NOTES
Scrubby is worked in two pieces which are sewn together to make a mitt to fit hand.

MITT (make 2)
Holding two strands of A together, cast on 22 sts.
Knit 10 rows.
Change to work in St st with 1 strand of B, work 6 rows.
Row 1 (Right Side): K1, k2tog, knit to last 3 sts, k2tog, k1.
Row 2: P1, p2tog, purl to last 3 sts, p2tog, p1.
Repeat last 2 rows until 6 sts remain on last row worked.
Last Row: [K2tog] 3 times – 3 sts.
Cut yarn, leaving a long tail for sewing. Thread tail through 3 sts and pull to gather. Secure end.

FINISHING
Sew pieces together along side edges, leaving cast-on edges unsewn.

HANGING LOOP
Holding two strands of A together, cast on 20 sts.
Knit 1 row.
Bind off, leaving a long tail for sewing.
Sew side edges together to make a loop. Sew on to top of Mitt.
Weave in ends.•

patriotic knit scrubby

Designed by Rebecca J. Venton

Easy

MATERIALS

Yarn (4)
RED HEART® Scrubby™, solids 3.5 oz (100 g), 92 yd (85 m), prints 3.0 oz (85 g) 78 yds (71 m) balls
• 1 ball each 905 Cherry A, 10 Coconut B and 870 Royal C

Needles
Susan Bates® Knitting Needles: 5mm [US 8]

Notions
4 stitch markers
Yarn needle

GAUGE

16 sts = 4" [10 cm]; 21 rows = 4" [10 cm] in Garter stitch. *CHECK YOUR GAUGE.* Use any size needles to obtain the gauge.

FINISHED SIZE

Star measures 8" x 8" (20 x 20 cm)

SPECIAL TECHNIQUE

kfb (knit into front and back): Knit next stitch but do not remove from needle, knit into back loop of same stitch and remove from needle.

LEARN BY VIDEO

www.go-crafty.com
kfb (knit into front and back of stitch)

NOTE

This project is worked back and forth in rows. Side edges are sewn together when Star is finished.

STAR CENTER

With A, cast on 5 sts.
Row 1: [Kfb] 5 times – 10 sts.
Row 2: K2, place first marker, k2, place 2nd marker, k2, place 3rd marker, k2, place 4th marker, k2.
Row 3: [Kfb] 10 times – 20 sts; 4 sts between each marker.
Row 4: Knit.
Row 5: Change to B, [kfb, knit to 1 st before marker, kfb, slip marker] 4 times, kfb, knit to last st, kfb – 30 sts.
Row 6: Knit.
Rows 7-10: Repeat Rows 5-6 – 50 sts at end of last row; 10 sts between each marker.
Rows 11-12: Change to C and repeat Rows 5-6 – 60 sts; 12 sts between each marker.

Shape First Star Point
Rows 1-2: K12, leave remaining sts unworked.
Row 3: K2tog, k8, k2tog – 10 sts.
Rows 4-5: Knit.
Row 6: K2tog, k6, k2tog – 8 sts.
Rows 7-8: Knit.
Row 9: K2tog, k4, k2tog – 6 sts.
Rows 10-11: Knit.
Row 12: K2tog, k2, k2tog – 4 sts.
Row 13: [K2tog] twice – 2 sts.
Row 14: K2tog – 1 st.
Fasten off last st.

Shape Second-Fourth Star Points
Join C in next unworked st of Star Center. Repeat Rows 1-14 of First Star Point.

Shape Fifth Star Point.
Work as for Second Star Point until Row 13 has been completed.

Shape Hanger
Row 14: Change to B and k2.
Repeat Row 14 until Hanger measures 3" [7.5 cm].
Bind off, leaving a long tail.

FINISHING

Sew side edges together to create Star. Fold bind-off row of Hanger to tip of point and, using long tail, sew in place. Weave in ends.•

picot edge knit washcloth

Designed by Bobbie Anderson

Easy

MATERIALS

Yarn
RED HEART® Scrubby Cotton®, solids 3.5 oz (100 g) 145 yd (133 m), prints 3 oz (85 g) 128 yd (117 m) balls
• 1 ball each: 7365 Tan A, 7230 Peachy B

Needles
Susan Bates® Knitting Needles:
4.5 mm [US 7] and 5mm [US 8]

Notions
Yarn needle

GAUGE
14.5 sts = 4"[10 cm]; 30 rows = 4" [10 cm] in Garter st.
Exact gauge is not crucial for this project.

FINISHED SIZE
Washcloth measures 7" [18 cm] wide x 7"[18 cm] long

SPECIAL TECHNIQUE
Picot Bind Off (Right Side): Bind off 2 sts; * slip remaining st from RH needle to LH needle, cast on 3 sts, bind off 5 sts; repeat from * across row.

WASHCLOTH
With larger needle and A, loosely cast on 24 stitches.
Work in Garter st until piece measures 6½" [16.5 cm], ending with a Wrong Side row.
Cut A.

BORDER
With smaller needle and B, knit 1 row.
Row 1 (Wrong Side): Purl.
Row 2 (Right Side): Work Picot Bind Off.
Fasten off last stitch.
Repeat Border on each of the remaining 3 edges, with Right Side facing, picking up and knitting
24 sts on each, and then working Rows 1 and 2.

FINISHING
Weave in all ends. •

small rosebud scrubby

Designed by Jodi Lewanda

Beginner

MATERIALS

Yarn
RED HEART® Scrubby™, solids 3.5 oz (100 g), 92 yd (85 m), prints 3.0 oz (85 g) 78 yds (71 m) balls
• 1 ball each 10 Coconut A, 215 Bamboo B, and 510 Glacier C

Needles
Susan Bates® Knitting Needles: 4mm [US 6]

FINISHED SIZE

Scrubby measures about 3» [7.5 cm] diameter.

Notions
Yarn needle

GAUGE

17 sts = 4" [10 cm]; 19 rows = 4" [10 cm] in Stockinette stitch (knit on right side, purl on wrong side). Gauge is not critical for this project.

NOTES

1 Scrubby is worked back and forth in rows of Stockinette stitch (knit on right side, purl on wrong side).
2 Stitches are bound off about every fourth row to form a slanting edge. The finished piece is rolled, beginning at narrow end and with slanting edge along top, to form rosebud.
3 Stitches are sewn at base of rolled rosebud to hold flower in place.

ROSEBUD (make 3—1 in each yarn color).
Cast on 72 sts.
Rows 1–4: Beginning with a right side row (knit), work in Stockinette stitch (knit on right side, purl on wrong side) for 4 rows.
Row 5 (right side): Bind off 20 sts, knit to end of row—52 sts.
Rows 6–8: Beginning with a wrong side row (purl), work in

Stockinette stitch for 3 rows.
Row 9: Bind off 18 sts, knit to end of row—34 sts.
Rows 10–12: Beginning with a wrong side row (purl), work in Stockinette stitch for 3 rows.
Row 13: Bind off 20 sts, knit to end of row—14 sts.
Row 14: Purl.
Bind off all remaining sts. Cut yarn, leaving a tail about 18" [45.5 cm] long for sewing.

FINISHING

Thread tail into yarn needle. With right side facing out and beginning at narrow end, loosely roll piece into a rosebud shape. Use tail to sew a few stitches at the base of the rosebud to hold the shape. Weave in ends.•

sweet kitty face scrubby

Designed by Michele Wilcox

● ●
Easy

MATERIALS

Yarn
RED HEART® Scrubby Sparkle™, solids 3 oz (85g), 174 yd (159m) balls
• 1 ball each 8417 Oyster A, 8012 Licorice B, and 8929 Strawberry C

Needles
Susan Bates® Knitting Needles:
3.75mm [US 5]

Notions
Buttonhole or carpet thread in grey or ecru
Sewing needle
Yarn needle

GAUGE

19 sts = 3¼" (8.5 cm); 12 rows = 1½" (4 cm). CHECK YOUR GAUGE. Use any size needles to obtain the gauge.

FINISHED SIZE

Scrubby measures 7" wide x 6" long (18 x 15 cm) down center.

SPECIAL TECHNIQUE

kfb (knit into front and back): Knit next stitch but do not remove from needle, knit into back loop of same stitch and remove from needle.

LEARN BY VIDEO

www.go-crafty.com
kfb (knit into front and back of stitch)

SCRUBBY

Head
Beginning at neck, with A, cast on 15 sts.
Row 1: Knit.
Row 2: K1, kfb, knit to last 2 sts, kfb, k1—17 sts.

Rows 3–6: Repeat Rows 1 and 2 twice—21 sts.
Row 7 and 8: Repeat Row 2—25 sts.
Rows 9–14: Repeat Rows 3–8—31 sts.
Rows 15 and 16: Repeat Rows 1 and 2—35 sts.
Knit every row until piece measures 4½» (11.5 cm) from beginning.
Next row: K1, k2tog, knit to last 3 sts, k2tog, k1—33 sts.
Next row:> Knit.
Next 5 rows: K1, k2tog, knit to last 3 sts, k2tog, k1—23 sts.

First Ear
Row 1: K8; leave remaining sts unworked, turn—8 sts.
Row 2: Knit 8 sts.
Row 3: K1, k2tog, k2, k2tog, k1—6 sts.
Row 4: Knit.
Row 5: K1, [k2tog] twice, k1—4 sts.
Row 6: Knit.
Row 7: [K2tog] twice—2 sts.
Row 8:: K2tog. Bind off.

2nd Ear
Join yarn in first unworked st of Row 1 of first ear, bind off first 7 sts.
Row 1: Knit each remaining st—8 sts.
Rows 2–8: Repeat Rows 2–8 of first ear. Bind off.

Eye (make 2)
With B, cast on 6 sts.
Row 1: Knit.
Row 2: [K2tog] 3 times—3 sts. Cut, leaving a long tail.
Thread tail on yarn needle, gather stitches of last row together, pull gently but tightly, and secure.

Tongue
With C, cast on 4 sts.
Rows 1–3: Knit. Cut, leaving a long tail.
Thread tail on yarn needle, gather stitches of last row together, pull gently but tightly, and secure.

Nose
With B, cast on 5 sts.
Work same as tongue.

FINISHING

With sewing needle and thread, sew pieces in place. Trim "eyelash" ends as needed to make facial features more distinct.
With B, refer to photograph as a guide and embroider mouth with back stitches.
Weave in ends.●

ghostly dish scrubber

Designed by Nancy Anderson

Easy

MATERIALS

Yarn 4
RED HEART® Scrubby™, solids 3.5 oz (100 g), 92 yd (85 m), prints 3.0 oz (85 g) 78 yds (71 m) balls
• 1 ball each 10 Coconut A and 12 Black B
Note Only a small quantity of B is needed for this project.

Needles
Susan Bates® Knitting Needles:
 5mm [US 8]

Notions
Yarn needle
2 stitch markers

GAUGE
16 sts = 4" (10 cm); 34 rows = 4" (10 cm. CHECK YOUR GAUGE. Use any size needles to obtain the gauge.

FINISHED SIZE
Scrubber measures 9½" across arms x 9¼" long (24 x 23.5 cm.)

SPECIAL TECHNIQUE
kfb (knit into front and back): Knit next stitch but do not remove from needle, knit into back loop of same stitch and remove from needle.

LEARN BY VIDEO
www.go-crafty.com
kfb (knit into front and back of stitch)

NOTES
1 Scrubby is worked back and forth in rows from head down in Garter st (knit every row).
2 Stitches are picked up across side edges to knit arms.

GHOST
With A, cast on 6 sts.

Row 1 (right side): K1, kfb, k2, kfb, k1—8 sts.
Row 2: K1, kfb, k4, kfb, k1—10 sts.
Row 3: K1, kfb, k6, kfb, k1—12 sts.
Row 4: K1, kfb, k8, kfb, k1—14 sts.
Row 5: K1, kfb, k10, kfb, k1—16 sts.
Rows 6–20: Knit.
Row 21: K1, k2tog, k10, k2tog, k1—14 sts.
Row 22: Knit.
Row 23: [K2, kfb] 4 times, k2—18 sts. Place marker at each end of row.
Row 24: *K2, kfb; repeat from * across—24 sts.
Rows 25–54: Knit.
Row 55: K1, k2tog, k18, k2tog, k1—22 sts.
Row 56: K1, k2tog, k16, k2tog, k1—20 sts.
Row 57: K1, k2tog, k14, k2tog, k1—18 sts.
Row 58: K1, k2tog, k12, k2tog, k1—16 sts.
Row 59: K1, k2tog, k11, kfb, k1.
Row 60: Knit.
Rows 61 and 62: Repeat Rows 59 and 60.
Row 63: Repeat Row 59.
Row 64: K1, kfb, k11, k2tog, k1.
Rows 65–67: Repeat Rows 61–63.
Row 68: K13, k2tog, k1—15 sts.
Row 69: K1, k2tog, k10, kfb, k1.
Row 70: K12, k2tog, k1—14 sts.
Row 71: K1, k2tog, k9, kfb, k1.
Row 72: K11, k2tog, k1—13 sts.
Row 73: K1, [k2tog, k1] 4 times—9 sts.
Bind off.

Right Arm
Row 1: With right side facing, beginning at marked row, pick up and knit 8 sts across ends of rows.
Rows 2–15: Work in Garter st for 14 rows.
Row 16: K1, k2tog, k2, k2tog, k1—6 sts.
Row 17: K1, [k2tog] twice, k1—4 sts.
Bind off.

Left Arm
Row 1: With wrong side facing, beginning at marked row, pick up and knit 8 sts across ends of rows.
Rows 2–17: Work same as right arm.

FINISHING
Using photograph as a guide, with B, embroider 3 or 4 vertical straight stitches for each eye and short, horizontal straight stitches for mouth. Pull stitches gently through piece so fabric doesn't pucker.
Weave in ends.•

striped knit scrubby mitt

Designed by Lorna Miser

Easy

MATERIALS

Yarn
RED HEART® Scrubby Cotton®, solids 3.5 oz (100 g) 145 yd (133 m), prints 3 oz (85 g) 128 yd (117 m) balls
• 1 ball each 7365 Tan A, 7105 Loofah B, 7230 Peachy C

Needles
Susan Bates® Knitting Needles: 4 mm [US 6]

Notions
Yarn needle

GAUGE
16 sts = 4" [10 cm]; 32 rows = 4" [10 cm] in Garter Stitch (knit every row). *CHECK YOUR GAUGE.* Use any size needle to obtain the gauge.

FINISHED SIZE
8½" in length x 9" in circumference [22 cm x 23 cm]

PATTERN STITCH
Garter Stitch
Row 1 (Right Side): K all sts.
Row 2 (Wrong Side): K all sts.
Repeat rows 1-2.

SPECIAL STITCH
k2tog: Knit two stitches together (decrease).

LEARN BY VIDEO
www.go-crafty.com
k2tog (knit 2 stitches together)

NOTES
Mitt is knit flat then seamed.
Carry yarn not in use up the side of work.

MITT
With A, cast on 32 sts.
Rows 1-2: With A, knit across row.
Rows 3-4:: Change to C and knit across row.
Rows 5-6: Change to B and knit across row.
Rows 7-8: Change to A and knit across row.
Rows 9-10: Change to B and knit across row.
Rows 11-12: Change to C and knit across row.
Repeat Rows 1-12 for stripe pattern until Mitt measures 6½" [16 cm] from cast on edge, ending after a Wrong Side row. Continue in stripe pattern and begin decrease rows as follows:
Next Row (Right Side): *K6, k2tog*; repeat from * to * across row—28 sts.
Next Row (Wrong Side): Knit across row.
Next Row: *K5, k2tog*; repeat from * to * across row—24 sts.
Next Row: Knit across row.
Next Row: *K4, k2tog*; repeat from * to * across row—20 sts.
Next Row: Knit across row.
Next Row: *K3, k2tog*; repeat from * to * across row—16 sts.
Next Row: Knit across row.
Next Row: *K2, k2tog*; repeat from * to * across row—12 sts.
Next Row: Knit across row.
Next Row: *K1, k2tog*; repeat from * to * across row—8 sts.
Next Row: Knit across row.
Cut a 20" [51 cm] long yarn tail. Thread tail through remaining 8 stitches, pull tightly to close and tie off.

FINISHING
Thread Yarn Needle with yarn tail and sew seam closed. Weave in ends.•

make it shine knit scrubby

Designed by Michele Maks

Easy

MATERIALS

Yarn (4)
RED HEART® Scrubby Cotton®, solids 3.5 oz (100 g) 145 yd (133 m), prints 3 oz (85 g) 128 yd (117 m) balls
• 1 ball each 934 Candy A, 709 Bubblegum B

Needles
Susan Bates® Knitting Needles:
6 mm [US 10]

Notions
Yarn needle

GAUGE

13 sts = 4" [10 cm]; 40 rows = 4" [10 cm] in Garter Stitch (knit every row). *CHECK YOUR GAUGE.* Use any size needle to obtain the gauge.

FINISHED SIZE

Scrubby measures: 4" x 4" in diameter [10 x 10 cm]

SPECIAL TECHNIQUES

k2tog Knit 2 sts together (decrease).
kfb (knit into front and back): Knit next stitch but do not remove from needle, knit into back loop of same stitch and remove from needle.
skp Slip 1, knit 1, pass slip stitch over (decrease).

LEARN BY VIDEO

www.go-crafty.com
k2tog (knit 2 stitches together)
kfb (knit into front and back of stitch)
skp (slip 1, knit 1, pass slip stitch over)

PATTERN STITCHES

Garter Stitch
Row 1 (Right Side): Knit all stitches.

Row 2 (Wrong Side): Knit all stitches.
Repeat Rows 1-2 for Garter Stitch.

NOTES

Spiraling knit strip form the "Base" for the Posey Scrubby. Contrasting "Centers" are knit separately and affixed to center of Scrubby on both sides.

SCRUBBY

Base
With A, cast on 26 sts.
Row 1 (Right Side): Skp, k23 sts, kfb—26 sts.
Row 2 (Wrong Side): Kfb, k23 sts, k2tog—26 sts.
Rows 3-44: Repeat Rows 1-2.
Row 45: Bind off all stitches in knit.
Fasten off leaving a 10" [26 cm] long yarn tail.

Seaming Scrubby Base and Closing Sides
Thread yarn needle with tail. Sew the bound off edge to the cast on edge matching up the diagonal ends and forming a tube. Fasten securely. With yarn needle and yarn, and using a running stitch, sew along the edge of the tube on one side. Gather the stitches together and pull tightly until the side is completely closed forming a circular puff. Fasten securely.
Repeat on opposite side of tube.
Set Scrubby Base aside.
With B, cast on 26 sts.
Row 1 (Right Side): Skp, k23 sts, kfb.
Row 2 (Wrong Side): Kfb, k23 sts, k2tog.
Rows 3-44: Repeat Rows 1-2.
Row 45: Bind off all stitches in Knit.
Fasten off leaving a 10" [26 cm] long yarn tail.
Repeat instructions for Seaming Scrubby Base and Closing Sides.

Center A (Make 2)
With A, cast on 4 sts.
Row 1 (Right Side): Kfb in each st across row—8 sts.
Row 2 (Wrong Side): Kfb in each st across row—16 sts.
Row 3: Kfb in each st across row—32 sts.
Row 4: Bind off all stitches loosely in knit.
Fasten off leaving a 10" [26 cm] long yarn tail.
Thread yarn needle with yarn tail and sew ends together. Pull tightly to form a circle and tie off. Sew one "Center" in A on each side of Posey Scrubby B.

Center B (Make 2)
With B, cast on 4 sts.
Row 1 (Right Side): Kfb in each st across row—8 sts.
Row 2 (Wrong Side): Kfb in each st across row—16 sts.
Row 3: Kfb in each st across row—32 sts.

Row 4: Bind off all stitches loosely in Knit.
Fasten off leaving a 10" [26 cm] long yarn tail. Thread Yarn
Needle with yarn tail and sew ends together. Pull tightly to
form a circle and tie off. Sew one "Center" in B on each side of

Posey Scrubby A.

FINISHING

Weave in ends.●

puppy scrubby

Designed by Michele Wilcox

Easy

MATERIALS

Yarn (4)
RED HEART® Scrubby™, solids 3.5 oz (100 g), 92 yd (85 m), prints 3.0 oz (85 g) 78 yds (71 m) balls
• 1 ball each 938 Almond A, 930 Marble B, and 10 Coconut C

Needles
Susan Bates® Knitting Needles: 3.75mm [US 5]

Notions
Small amount of black yarn
Yarn needle

GAUGE
 Gauge is not critical for this project.

FINISHED SIZE
Scrubby measures 6½" [16.5 cm] x 6½" [16.5 cm].

SPECIAL TECHNIQUE
kfb (knit into front and back): Knit next stitch but do not remove from needle, knit into back loop of same stitch and remove from needle.

LEARN BY VIDEO
www.go-crafty.com
kfb (knit into front and back of stitch)

PUPPY FACE
With A, cast on 34 sts.
Row 1: [K1, p1] across.
Repeat Row 1 until piece measures 6½" [16.5 cm] from beginning. Bind off in pattern.

EAR (Make 2)
With B, cast on 6 sts.
Rows 1-4: Knit.
Row 5: K1, kfb, k2, kfb, k1 – 8 sts.
Row 6: Knit.
Repeat Row 6 until piece measures 3¾" [9.5 cm] from beginning.
Next Row: K1, k2tog, k2, k2tog, k1 – 6 sts.
Next Row: Knit.
Next Row: K1, [k2tog] 2 times, k1 – 4 sts.
Next Row: [K2tog] 2 times – 2 sts.
Next Row: K2tog.
Fasten off, leaving a long end.

HANGER
With A, cast on 16 sts.
Bind off.
Fold in half, lining up ends. Sew ends in center of top of Face.

SNOUT
With C, cast on 5 sts.
Row 1: Knit.
Row 2: Kfb, knit to last st, kfb – 7 sts.
Row 3: Knit.
Rows 4-7: Repeat Rows 2-3 – 11 sts at end of Row 7.
Rows 8-10: Knit.
Row 11: K2tog, knit to last 2 sts, k2tog – 9 sts.
Rows 12-15: Repeat Rows 10-11 – 5 sts at end of Row 15.
Bind off, leaving long end of yarn.

FINISHING
Sew ears on either side of Puppy Face. Using Black, embroider nose and eyes in satin stitch on Snout. Embroider mouth in straight stitch. Sew Snout in center of Face.
Weave in ends.•

polar bear scrubby mitt

Designed by Rebecca J. Venton

Easy

MATERIALS

Yarn

RED HEART® Scrubby Sparkle™, solids 3 oz (85g), 174 yd (159m) balls
• 1 ball each 8929 Strawberry A, 8690 Avocado B, 8001 Marshmallow C, 8012 Licorice D

Needles
Susan Bates® Knitting Needles: 5mm [US 8]

Notions
Yarn needle

GAUGE
18 sts = 4" [10 cm]; 24 rows = 4" [10 cm] in Garter Stitch (knit every row). Gauge is not critical for this pattern. *CHECK YOUR GAUGE.* Use any size needle to obtain the gauge.

SPECIAL TECHNIQUES
kfb (knit into front and back): Knit next stitch but do not re-move from needle, knit into back loop of same stitch and remove from needle.
k2tog: Knit 2 stitches together (decrease).

LEARN BY VIDEO
www.go-crafty.com
kfb (knit into front and back of stitch)
k2tog (knit 2 stitches together)

NOTES
1 Carry yarn not in use up side of work unless otherwise instructed.
2 For facial features, use photo as a guide

MITT (make 2)
With A, cast on 27 sts.

Rows 1-2: With A, knit.
Rows 3-4: With B, knit.
Repeat Rows 1-4, four times.
Rows 21-24: With A, knit. At end of Row 24, fasten off yarn, change to C.
Rows 25-33: With C, knit.
Row 34: K2tog, knit to last 2 sts, k2tog—25 sts.
Rows 35-38: With C, knit.
Row 39: K2tog, knit to last 2 sts, k2tog—23 sts.
Rows 40-43: With C, knit.
Row 44: K2tog, knit to last 2 sts, k2tog—21 sts.
Rows 45-48: With C, knit.
Row 49: K2tog, knit to last 2 sts, k2tog—19 sts.
Row 50: Bind off all sts.

EARS (make 2)
With C, cast on 3 stitches.
Row 1: Kfb in first and last stitch—5 sts.
Rows 2-3: Knit.
Row 4: Kfb in first and last stitch—7 sts.
Rows 5-6: Knit.
Row 7: Kfb in first and last stitch—9 sts.
Row 8: Bind off all sts. Cut yarn leaving a tail 15" [38 cm] long for attaching Ears.

NOSE
With D, cast on 6 stitches.
Row 1: Knit.
Row 2: K2tog, K2, K2tog—4 sts.
Row 3: K2tog, K2tog—2 sts.
Row 4: Bind off all sts. Cut yarn leaving a tail 15" [38 cm] long for attaching Nose and embroidering "Mouth".

FINISHING
With right side facing, using Yarn Needle and A and C, seam Mitt together.

EARS
With yarn needle and C, sew ears to top corners of Mitt.
NOSE
With yarn needle and D, sew nose to top center of Mitt over C. Sew to top layer only of Mitt.
MOUTH
With yarn needle and D, embroider mouth on Mitt over C, centering mouth under the nose.
EYES
With yarn needle and D, embroider eyes on Mitt over C, centering eyes above nose.
Weave in all ends.•

knit halloween scrubby

Designed by Sara Louise Greer

Easy

MATERIALS

Yarn (4)
RED HEART® Scrubby Sparkle™, solids 3 oz (85g), 174 yd (159m) balls

- 1 ball each 8570 Grape A, 8690 Avocado B, 8012 Licorice C

Needles
Susan Bates® Knitting Needles:
5mm [US 8]

Notions
Yarn needle

GAUGE

Gauge is not critical for this project.

FINISHED SIZE

Mitt measures 5" [12.5 cm] wide by 7½" [19 cm] long.

NOTES

Scrubby is worked in two pieces which are sewn together to make a mitt to fit hand.
Front is worked in intarsia, using a separate ball of yarn for each large block of color. Pick up new yarn from under old to twist yarns and prevent holes. Carry colors not in use loosely along wrong side of work.

BACK

With A, cast on 24 sts.
Knit 10 rows.
Change to St st and work 12 rows, end with a wrong side row.
Decrease Row 1 (Right Side): K1, k2tog, knit to last 3 sts, k2tog, k1 – 22 sts.
Work in St st for 7 rows.
Repeat Decrease Row 1 – 20 sts.
Work in St st for 3 rows.
Change to B and repeat Decrease Row 1 – 18 sts.
Work in St st for 4 rows.

Decrease Row 2 (Wrong Side): P1, p2tog, purl to last 3 sts, p2tog, p1 – 16 sts.
Work in St st for 2 more rows. Cut B.
Change to A and work in St st for 4 rows.
Repeat Decrease Row 1 – 14 sts.
Work in St st for 3 rows.
Repeat last 4 rows 4 more times – 6 sts remain on last row worked.
Last Row: [K2tog] 3 times – 3 sts.
Cut yarn, leaving a long tail for sewing. Thread tail through 3 sts and pull to gather. Secure end.

FRONT

With A, cast on 24 sts.
Knit 10 rows.
Change to St st and work 12 rows, end with a wrong side row.
Decrease Row 1 (Right Side): K1, k2tog, knit to last 3 sts, k2tog, k1 – 22 sts.
Work in St st for 7 rows.

Buckle
Row 1 (Right Side): With A, k1, k2tog, k3, change to C, k10, change to A, k3, k2tog, k1 – 20 sts.
Rows 2 and 4: With A, p5, with C, p10, with A, p5.
Row 3: K5 with A, k10 with C, k5 with A. Cut A.
Row 5: Change to B, k1, k2tog, k2, k3 with C, change to B, k4, k3 with C, change to B, k2, k2tog, k1 – 18 sts.
Row 6: P4 with B, p3 with C, p4 with B, p3 with C, p4 with B.
Rows 7 and 9: K4 with B, k3 with C, k4 with B, k3 with C, k4 with B.
Row 8: P4 with B, p3 with C, p4 with B, p3 with C, p4 with B.
Row 10: With B, p1, p2tog, p1, with C, k3, with B, k4, with C, k3, with B, p1, p2tog, p1 – 16 sts
Row 11: K3 with B, k3 with C, k4 with B, k3 with C, k3 with B.
Row 12: P3 with B, p3 with C, p4 with B, p3 with C, p3 with B. Cut B.
Rows 13 and 15: K4 with A, k10 with C, k4 with A.
Rows 14 and 16: P4 with A, p10 with C, p4 with A. Cut C.
Decrease Row 1 (Right Side): Working with A only, k1, k2tog, knit to last 3 sts, k2tog, k1 – 14 sts.
Work in St st for 3 rows.
Repeat last 4 rows 4 more times – 6 sts remain on last row worked.
Last Row: [K2tog] 3 times – 3 sts.
Cut yarn, leaving a long tail for sewing. Thread tail through 3 sts and pull to gather. Secure end.

FINISHING

Sew pieces together along side edges, leaving cast-on edges unsewn.

Hanging Loop
Holding two strands of B together, cast on 20 sts. Knit 1 row.
Bind off, leaving a long tail for sewing.
Sew side edges together to make a loop. Sew on to top of Mitt.
Weave in ends. •

sly fox scrubby

Designed by Rebecca J. Venton

Easy

MATERIALS

Yarn (4)
RED HEART® Scrubby Sparkle™, solids 3 oz (85g), 174 yd (159m) balls
• 1 ball each 8260 Orange A, 8001 Marshmallow B, and 8012 Licorice C

Needles
Susan Bates® Knitting Needles:
5mm [US 8]

Notions
Yarn needle

GAUGE

Gauge is not critical for this project.

SPECIAL TECHNIQUE

kfb (knit into front and back): Knit next stitch but do not remove from needle, knit into back loop of same stitch and remove from needle.
Scrubby measures 6" [15 cm] wide x 8" [20.5 cm] long

LEARN BY VIDEO

www.go-crafty.com
kfb (knit into front and back of stitch)

BODY

With A, cast on 26 sts.
Knit every row until piece measures 2" [5 cm] from beginning.
Change to B and knit every row for 2" [5 cm] more.
Change to A and knit every row for 2" [5 cm] more.
Bind off.

NOSE

With A, cast on 12 sts.
Row 1: Knit.
Row 2: K2tog, k8, k2tog – 10 sts.
Row 3: Knit.
Row 4: K2tog, k6, k2tog – 8 sts.
Row 5: Knit.

Row 6: K2tog, k4, k2tog – 6 sts.
Row 7: Knit.
Row 8: K2tog, k2, k2tog – 4 sts.
Row 9: Knit.
Row 10: [K2tog] twice – 2 sts.
Row 11: Knit.
Row 12: K2tog.
Fasten off, leaving long tail for sewing.

EAR (Make 2)

Outer Ear
With A, cast on 10 sts.
Rows 1-4: Knit.
Row 5: K2tog, k6, k2tog – 8 sts.
Row 6: Knit.
Row 7: K2tog, k4, k2tog – 6 sts.
Row 8: Knit.
Row 9: K2tog, k2, k2tog – 4 sts.
Row 10: Knit.
Row 11: [K2tog] twice – 2 sts.
Row 12: K2tog.
Fasten off, leaving long tail for sewing.

Inner Ear
With B, cast on 8 sts.
Rows 1-3: Knit.
Row 4: K2tog, k4, k2tog – 6 sts.
Row 5: Knit.
Row 6: K2tog, k2, k2tog – 4 sts.
Row 7: Knit.
Row 8: [K2tog] twice – 2 sts.
Row 9: K2tog.
Fasten off, leaving long tail for sewing.

EYE(Make 2)

With C, cast on 3 sts.
Row 1: Kfb, k1, kfb – 5 sts.
Row 2: Knit.
Row 3: K2tog, k1, k2tog – 3 sts.
Bind off, leaving long tail for sewing.

NOSE TIP (Make 1)

Work same as for Eye.

FINISHING

Following photo, position and sew Inner Ear to Outer Ear.
Sew one Ear to either side of Body.
Sew Nose to Body. Sew Eyes and Nose Tip to Body.
Weave in ends.•

holiday mitten scrubby

Designed by Michele Wilcox

Easy

MATERIALS

Yarn (4)
RED HEART® Scrubby™, solids 3.5 oz (100 g), 92 yd (85 m), prints 3.0 oz (85 g) 78 yds (71 m) balls
• 1 ball each 10 Coconut A, and 905 Cherry B

Needles
Susan Bates® Knitting Needles: 4mm [US 6]

Notions
Two stitch markers
Two stitch holders
Yarn needle

GAUGE
Gauge is not critical for this project.

FINISHED SIZE
Scrubby measures about 4½" [11.5 cm] across hand and 8½" [21.5 cm] long, not including hanging loop.

SPECIAL TECHNIQUE
kfb (knit into front and back): Knit next stitch but do not remove from needle, knit into back loop of same stitch and remove from needle.

LEARN BY VIDEO
www.go-crafty.com
kfb (knit into front and back of stitch)

NOTES
1 Mitt is worked from wrist edge upwards, back and forth in rows.
2 Stitches are increased to shape thumb gusset then stitches are divided onto holders, leaving the thumb stitches to be worked separately. After thumb is complete, the held stitches are returned to the needles and the remainder of the hand is knit.
3 Side edges of mitt are sewn together to complete piece.

MITTEN

Cuff
Beginning at wrist edge, with A, cast on 30 sts.
Work in Garter stitch (knit every row) until piece measures about 1½" [4 cm] from beginning.

Lower Hand
Change to B.
Row 1: (right side): [K9, kfb] 3 times—33 sts.
Rows 2–6: Work in Garter stitch for 5 rows.

Shape Thumb Gusset
Row 1 (right side): K15, place marker, kfb, k1, kfb, place marker, k15—35 sts (5 sts between markers).
Row 2: Knit, slipping markers as you come to them.
Row 3: Knit to first marker, slip marker, kfb, knit to 1 st before next marker, kfb, slip marker, knit to end of row—37 sts (7 sts between markers).
Rows 4–9: Repeat Rows 2 and 3 three times—43 sts (13 sts between markers).
Row 10: Knit, slipping markers as you come to them.
Row 11: K15 and place these sts on a holder, remove marker, k13, remove marker, place remaining 15 sts on a 2nd holder—13 sts remain on needle for thumb.

Thumb
Work in Garter stitch over 13 thumb sts only for 10 rows.
Decrease Row: [K2tog] 3 times, k1, [k2tog] 3 times—7 sts.
Cut yarn, leaving a long tail for sewing. Weave tail through the seven thumb stitches remaining on needle and pull tight. Sew side edges of thumb together.

Upper Hand
With right side facing, return the 15 sts from holder before thumb (the sts that have already been knit) onto the right needle. Place the 15 sts from the 2nd holder onto the left needle. With the left needle, pick up and k3 sts across base of thumb, knit the remaining 15 sts from left needle—33 sts.
Work in Garter stitch until B-colored section of piece measures about 6" [15 cm].
Next Row: [K1, k2tog] 11 times—22 sts.
Next Row: Knit.
Next Row: [K2tog] 11 times—11 sts.
Cut yarn, leaving a long tail for sewing. Weave tail through stitches remaining on needle and pull tight. Sew side edges of hand and cuff together, changing yarn color as needed to match color of edges.

HANGING LOOP
With A, cast on 16 sts.

Knit 1 row.

Bind off, leaving a long tail for sewing. Fold hanging loop in half and sew ends to top of cuff on side opposite thumb.

FINISHING
Weave in ends.•

school of scrubby knit fish

Designed by Michele Wilcox

Easy

MATERIALS

Yarn 4

RED HEART® Scrubby™, solids 3.5 oz (100 g), 92 yd (85 m), prints 3.0 oz (85 g) 78 yds (71 m) balls

• 1 ball each 905 Cherry, 501 Ocean, 241 Duckie, and 620 Lime

Needles
Susan Bates® Knitting Needles:
4.5mm [US 7]

Notions
Small amount of black yarn
Yarn needle

GAUGE
Gauge is not critical for this project.

FINISHED SIZE
Scrubby measures 9" [23 cm] across from tip of mouth to tip of tail.

SPECIAL TECHNIQUE
kfb (knit into front and back): Knit next stitch but do not remove from needle, knit into back loop of same stitch and remove from needle.

LEARN BY VIDEO
www.go-crafty.com
kfb (knit into front and back of stitch)

FISH
With desired color and beginning at mouth, cast on 6 sts.
Rows 1-3: Knit.
Row 4: K2tog, k2, k2tog – 4 sts.

Row 5: Knit.
Row 6: K1, [kfb] twice, k1 – 6 sts.
Row 7: K1, kfb, knit to last 2 sts, kfb, k1 – 8 sts.
Rows 8-12: Repeat Row 7 – 18 sts on last row worked.
Row 13: Knit.
Rows 14-17: Repeat Row 7 – 26 sts on last row worked.
Row 18: Knit.
Rows 19-20: Repeat Row 7 – 30 sts on last row worked.
Knit every row until piece measures 4" [10 cm] from beginning.

Shape Bottom Fin
Next Row: Cast on 5 sts, knit all sts to end of row – 35 sts.
Knit 1 row.
Next Row: Bind off 5 sts, knit to end of row – 30 sts.
Knit every row until piece measures 5" [12.5 cm] from beginning, end with Bottom Fin at end of row.

Shape Top Fin
Next Row: Cast on 5 sts, knit all sts to end of row – 35 sts.
Knit 5 rows.
Next Row: K2tog, knit to end of row – 34 sts.
Next Row: Knit.
Next Row: K2tog, knit to end of row – 33 sts.
Next Row: Knit.
Next Row: K2tog, knit to end of row – 32 sts.
Next Row: Knit.
Next Row: Bind off 2 sts, knit to end of row – 30 sts.
Next Row: K1, k2tog, knit to last 3 sts, k2tog, k1 – 28 sts.
Repeat last row 8 more times – 12 sts on last row worked.

Shape Tail
Next Row: Kfb in each st across – 24 sts.
Knit every row until Tail measures 2" [5 cm].
Bind off.

Side Fin (make 2)
Cast on 10 sts.
Rows 1-4: Knit.
Row 5: K2tog, knit to last 2 sts, k2tog – 8 sts.
Row 6: Knit.
Row 7: Repeat Row 5 – 6 sts.
Row 8: Knit.
Row 9: Repeat Row 5 – 4 sts.
Bind off.

FINISHING
Sew Side Fins in center of either side of Fish. Weave in ends. With black yarn, embroider an eye on each side in satin stitch. •

scrubby swim trunks

Designed by Jody Lewanda

Easy

MATERIALS

Yarn ④

RED HEART® Scrubby™, solids 3.5 oz (100 g), 92 yd (85 m), prints 3.0 oz (85 g) 78 yds (71 m) balls
• 1 ball each 501 Ocean A, 10 Coconut B, 940 Capri C

Needles
Susan Bates® Knitting Needles:
4.5 mm [US 7]

Hooks
Susan Bates® Crochet Hook:
4mm [G-6]

Notions
Stitch Holder
Yarn needle

GAUGE
17 sts = 4" [10 cm]; 19 rows = 4" [10 cm] in Stockinette Stitch. Gauge is not critical for this pattern. *CHECK YOUR GAUGE.* Use any size needle to obtain the gauge.

FINISHED SIZE
Scrubby Swim Trunks measure: 6¼" [16 cm] long x 6" [15 cm] wide.

PATTERN STITCH
Stockinette Stitch
Row 1 (Right Side): Knit.
Row 2 (Wrong Side): Purl.
Repeat Rows 1-2 for Stockinette Stitch.

SPECIAL TECHNIQUE
k2tog: Knit 2 stitches together (decrease).

LEARN BY VIDEO
www.go-crafty.com
k2tog (knit 2 stitches together)

SCRUBBY SWIM TRUNKS
With A, cast on 25 sts.
Row 1 (Right Side): *K1, P1*, repeat from * to * to last stitch, K1.
Row 2 (Wrong Side): *P1, K1*; repeat from * to * to last stitch, P1.
Row 3 (Right Side): Repeat Row 1.
Cut yarn and change to B.
Row 4 (Wrong Side): With B, purl to end of row.
Row 5 (Right Side): With B, knit to end of row. Cut yarn and change to A.
Row 6 (Wrong Side): With A, purl to end of row.
Rows 7-8: Repeat Rows 1-2.
Row 9 (Right Side): Repeat Row 1.
Cut yarn and change to C.
Row 10 (Wrong Side): With C, purl to end of row.
Continue in Stockinette Stitch (knit on Right Side, purl on Wrong Side) with C until piece measures 4¼" [11 cm] from cast on edge, ending with a Wrong Side Row.

LEG SHAPING
Right Leg
Row 1 (Right Side): K12; place remaining 13 stitches on Stitch Holder. Turn work.
Row 2 (Wrong Side): Purl to end of row.
Rows 3-4: Work in Stockinette Stitch as established.
Row 5 (Right Side): K10, K2tog—11 sts.
Rows 6-8: Work in Stockinette Stitch as established.
Row 9 (Right Side): K9, K2tog—10 sts.
Rows 10-12: Work in Stockinette Stitch as established.
Next Row (Right Side): Loosely bind off all stitches.

Left Leg
With Right Side facing, place 13 stitches from Stitch Holder on to knitting needle and join C.
Row 1 (Right Side): Bind off 1 stitch; knit to end of row—12 sts.
Row 2 (Wrong Side): Purl to end of row.
Rows 3-4: Work in Stockinette Stitch as established
Row 5 (Right Side): K2tog, K10—11 sts.
Rows 6-8: Work in Stockinette Stitch as established
Row 9 (Right Side): K2tog, K9—10 sts.
Rows 10-12: Work in Stockinette Stitch as established.
Next Row (Right Side): Loosely bind off all stitches.

WAIST CORD
With Crochet Hook and B, loosely chain 30 stitches or desired length of tie. Fasten off securely.

FINISHING
Using Yarn Needle, weave in all ends.
With Crochet Hook, run Waist Cord through the center of waist stripe (see photograph for placement), tie Cord in a bow on center front of Swim Trunks.•

decorate your tree scrubby

Designed by Michele Wilcox

Easy

MATERIALS

Yarn (4)
RED HEART® Scrubby™, solids 3.5 oz (100 g), 92 yd (85 m), prints 3.0 oz (85 g) 78 yds (71 m) balls
• 1 ball each 620 Lime A, 905 Cherry B and 241 Ducky C

Needles
Susan Bates® Knitting Needles:
3.75mm [US 5]

Notions
Yarn needle
Sewing needle and matching sewing thread

GAUGE
Gauge is not critical for this project.

FINISHED SIZE
Tree measures 9½" [23.5 cm] tall x 5½" [14 cm] at widest point.

NOTES
Each part of the scrubby is made separately, then the pieces are sewn together.

SPECIAL TECHNIQUES
k3tog: Knit 3 sts together.
kfb (knit into front and back): Knit 1 front and back (increase) Knit next st, then knit it through back loop.

LEARN BY VIDEO
www.go-crafty.com
k3tog (knit 3 stitches together)
kfp (knit into front and back of stitch)

TREE
Top of Tree
With A, cast on 3 sts.
Row 1: [Kfb] in each st—6 sts.
Row 2: Kfb, knit to last st, kfb—8 sts.
Row 3: Knit.
Rows 4-11: Repeat Rows 2-3—16 sts on last row worked.Z
Rows 12-13: K2tog, knit to last 2 sts, k2tog—12 sts on last row worked.
Row 14: Knit.
Rows 15-17: Repeat Row 2—18 sts on last row worked.
Row 18: Knit.
Rows 19-20: Repeat Row 12—14 sts on last row worked.
Row 21: Knit.
Rows 22-56: Repeat Rows 15-21 for 5 more times—24 sts on last row worked.
Rows 57-59: Repeat Rows 15-17—28 sts on last row worked.
Row 60: Knit.
Bind off.

TREE STAND
With B, cast on 15 sts.
Knit every row until piece measures 1½" [4 cm].
Rows 1-4: K2tog, knit to last 2 sts, k2tog—7 sts on last row worked.
Bind off, leaving a long end.
Center last row along last row of Tree and sew pieces together using long end.

HANGER
With C, cast on 12 sts.
Bind off, leaving a long end.
Fold in half and sew ends together. Center ends along first row of Tree and sew pieces together.

BALLS
(make 8 with B and 7 with C)
Leaving a long tail, cast on 5 sts.
Rows 1-3: Knit.
Row 4: K2tog, k1, k2tog—3 sts.
Row 5: K3tog.
Fasten off, leaving a long end.
Thread long end through all corners and pull to gather in a ball.
Secure end. Sew balls on Tree with matching sewing thread.

FINISHING
Weave in ends.•

sea monster bath puppet

Designed by Michele Wilcox

Easy

MATERIALS

Yarn

RED HEART® Scrubby™, solids 3.5 oz (100 g), 92 yd (85 m), prints 3.0 oz (85 g) 78 yds (71 m) balls
• 1 ball each 620 Lime A, 905 Cherry B, 10 Coconut C, 12 Black D, and 501 Ocean E

Needles
Susan Bates® Knitting Needles:
4mm [US 6]

Notions
Stitch holder
Yarn needle

GAUGE

Gauge is not critical for this project.

FINISHED SIZE

Puppet measures 14" (35.5 cm) including tail.

PATTERN STITCH

1 x 1 Rib (multiple of 2 sts)
Row 1 (right side): *K1, p1; repeat from * to end of row.
Repeat this row for 1 x 1 Rib.

SPECIAL TECHNIQUE

kfb (Knit into front and back): Knit next stitch but do not remove from needle, knit into back loop of same stitch and remove from needle.
k3tog: Knit next 3 stitches together.

> ### LEARN BY VIDEO
> www.go-crafty.com
> kfb (knit into front and back of stitch)
> k3tog (knit 3 stitches together)

NOTES

1 Puppet is made of glove, facial features, and tail.
2 Refer to photograph for placement of facial features and tail. All pieces are sewn to glove.

PUPPET

Glove
Beginning at wrist, with A, cast on 26 sts.
Work in 1 x 1 Rib until piece measures 5" (12.5 cm) from beginning.
Next Row: *[K1, p1] 6 times, kfb*, slide these 14 sts to stitch holder; repeat from * to * once—14 sts remain on needle.

Head Side 1
Work over 14 sts that remain on needle only.
Work in 1 x 1 Rib until piece measures 8" (20.5 cm) from beginning.
Next row: [K2tog] 7 times—7 sts. Cut yarn, leaving a long tail. Thread tail on needle. Slide sts onto yarn needle, pull tail tightly to gather, and secure.

Head Side 2
Return 14 sts on holder to needle. Work same as head side 1.

Inner Mouth (make 2)
With B, cast on 14 sts.
Work in 1 x 1 Rib until piece measures 3" (7.5 cm) from beginning.
Next row: [K2tog] 7 times—7 sts.
Cut yarn, leaving a long tail. Thread tail on needle. Slide sts onto yarn needle, pull tail tightly to gather, and secure.
Sew cast on edges of inner mouths together. Sew inner mouths to head sides. Sew sides of glove together. Turn piece right side out, so that seams are on the inside of glove.

Teeth (make 2)
With A, cast on 36 sts.
Knit 2 rows.

sea monster bath puppet

Change to C.

Knit 2 rows.

Bind off, leaving a long tail for sewing.

Position A-colored row of one set of teeth along edge of head slightly above mouth. Sew to head. Position A-colored row of other set of teeth along edge of head slightly below mouth. Sew to head, then sew short edges of teeth together. Pull tails to wrong side of piece.

Eye (make 2)

With C, cast on 6 sts.

Row 1: [Kfb] 6 times—12 sts.

Row 2: Knit.

Bind off, leaving a long tail for sewing. Gather sts through cast on edge and sew side edges together.

Pupil (make 2)

With D, cast on 1 st.

Row 1: (K1, p1, k1) in st—3 sts.

Row 2: K3tog—1 st.

Cut yarn, leaving a long tail. Pull tail through last st. Sew to center of eye, then sew eye in place.

Nostril (make 2)

With A, cast on 6 sts.

Knit 3 rows.

Cut yarn, leaving a long tail. Thread tail on needle. Slide sts onto yarn needle, pull tail tightly to gather, and secure. Weave tail around edges and pull tightly to form a cupped shape. Sew in place.

Spine

With E, cast on 40 sts.

Knit 2 rows.

Bind off. Center spine on back of glove, placing one end below eyes; pin in place, allowing lower section of spine to hang freely. Sew through top half of glove only.

Tail Fin (make 2)

With E, cast on 3 sts.

Row 1: Knit.

Row 2: Kfb in each st across—6 sts.

Rows 3 and 4: Repeat Rows 1 and 2—12 sts.

Knit every row until piece measures 2" (5 cm) from beginning.

Next row: [K2tog] 6 times—6 sts.

Bind off, leaving a long tail for sewing. Weave yarn through last row, gather sts, and sew fin to end of spine.

Side Fin (make 2)

With A, cast on 12 sts.

Row 1: Knit.

Row 2: K2tog, k to end of row—11 sts.

Rows 3–20: Repeat last 2 rows 9 times—2 sts.

Row 21: K2tog—1 st.

Cut yarn, leaving a long tail. Pull tail through last st. Sew in place on side of glove.

FINISHING

Weave in ends.●